D0773166

The Phoenix Living Poets

———⟨∞∞∞∞∞⟩———

BARE WIRES

Poets Published in
The Phoenix Living Poets Series

★

JAMES AITCHISON
ALEXANDER BAIRD · ALAN BOLD
R. H. BOWDEN · FREDERICK BROADIE
GEORGE MACKAY BROWN
HAYDEN CARRUTH · JOHN COTTON
JENNIFER COUROUCLI
GLORIA EVANS DAVIES
PATRIC DICKINSON
TOM EARLEY · D. J. ENRIGHT
IRENE FEKETE
JOHN FULLER · DAVID GILL
PETER GRUFFYDD
J. C. HALL · MOLLY HOLDEN
JOHN HORDER · P. J. KAVANAGH
RICHARD KELL · LAURIE LEE
LAURENCE LERNER
CHRISTOPHER LEVENSON
EDWARD LOWBURY · NORMAN MACCAIG
ROY McFADDEN
JON MANCHIP WHITE
JAMES MERRILL · RUTH MILLER
LESLIE NORRIS · ROBERT PACK
ARNOLD RATTENBURY
ADRIENNE RICH · JON SILKIN
JON STALLWORTHY
GILLIAN STONEHAM
EDWARD STOREY · TERENCE TILLER
SYDNEY TREMAYNE
LOTTE ZURNDORFER

BARE WIRES

by

PHILIP CALLOW

CHATTO AND WINDUS

THE HOGARTH PRESS

1972

Published by
Chatto and Windus Ltd
with The Hogarth Press Ltd
42 William IV Street
London W.C.2

*

Clarke, Irwin & Co. Ltd
Toronto

Distributed in the United States of America
by Wesleyan University Press

ISBN 0 8195 7042 7

ISBN 0 7011 1886 5

© Philip Callow 1972

Printed in Great Britain by
Lewis Reprints Ltd
London and Tonbridge

CONTENTS

THE BLUE LANTERN

I'll do the honours,
you say the word;
pictures in the hallway,
songs that you never heard.

I'll make the signals;
stand under the sky
on the roof wide open
with my astounded heart and eye.

I'll dance up naked
waving a shy grin:
frighten them all away,
only let lovers in.

I'll tend the plants
while you just stand;
flowers in the air of rooms,
sweetness springing from your hand.

I'll watch at the window;
lights will wink and move.
O such emptiness lapping
at the blue lantern of love.

DANCING BY THE RIVER

I'm afraid of time stopping
before I've mastered the rhythm.
Life opens in a dream
of slow rivers and your mother
always there in the warm kitchen.
Everything needs slowing up!
The Marx Brothers are on TV,
Corporation busmen have come out
but the cars give lifts
like they did in the war.
A picture postcard floats in
from the summit of Snowdon.
In three weeks I'll be cramming
through college —
and what I should be learning
is how to dance. Slowly.
Dancing by the river,
and to hell with reality.
In the dream and young,
majesty on the fields
and the direct message to the heart
from lips and eyes —
then I could do it.

MEDIA

There we were
mixed in messily with kids,
paintings alight on hut walls,
a shuffle of photographs on the floor

and this glinting claptrap
batted to and fro
like a blind eyeball nobody needed.
There I sat drinking tea,

my back to the flimsy wall
feeling the punched fists of wind,
glancing out now and then
at the beach's wild white apron,

at the abandon of gulls —
and then I knew it was a quarrel.
Poetry and music don't mix
any more than oil and water —

right or wrong
it was the flat arrogance of it,
the irrelevant tidiness
that set my sea crashing.

What kind of blindness is it
that has to separate media,
when the gales, the pictures,
tears of children,

artist kneeling by photographs
and his wife stirring tea
are all in the mad gamut
of this planet's mix-up?

NOTHING SPECIAL

Dropping in by chance,
passing through the empty afternoon,
not surprised to find you gone;

your lover drunk with sleep,
still in bed after a late party,
propping himself up to greet me

in the big communal room
where the life drifts and ebbs,
young men and girls meaning

nothing special to each other,
who are strangers to me.
I sit watching and listening,

thinking how good to be young
when you can stay here or go
and no questions asked;

nothing matters, the world
can lie in ruins outside the windows.
Let it go, while a girl is making tea.

TENEMENTS

It could be tenements in Naples —
except for the weather,
the Assistance.
And all that iron.
Bars rising, crossing,
iron landings, iron ladders,
a hard grid facing the sea,
a cage for living in —
it could be Alcatraz
except for the washing,
which decorates it all over,
every day
from top to bottom.
The whole structure flaps like a flag.

QUESTIONS

She casts a simple question,
lazily, combing her damp
mermaid hair.
And as he plunges in,
too deep,
talking with such vehemence,
agonising,
opening his mouth soundlessly
between thoughts
like a fish on the beach

      she marvels
at her washed hair,
the auburn tints
and the darkness lost down the sink,
wondering vaguely
why nothing is ever simple for him.

GIRL IN A ROOM

A girl of fourteen
in a room
with two men:
the men looking and not looking,
the girl shy and not shy,
suddenly years older
in this forcing house
of male awareness;
the men hovering wryly
between youth and fatherhood.
One jokes,
drags down his sweater
for a mini-skirt,
skylarks;
the other stares out
thoughtfully
through his bifocals

    while the girl
as if hiding in her hair
seems to be considering
both these solutions.

PRINT

No, not a man
because you said
'Here's Auntie Pearl.'
The sculptured profile
divides the print,
the opaque disc of her specs
fixed over the grained nose
bored out from underneath,
a black tunnel —

the chin leathery,
losing its tired lines
in a scrabble of grey fusewire
above the goitre

a bludgeoned, Black Country face,
ashy as a wasteground,
which the smile quietly contradicts.

EASTER

The wind sharp over the blue water.
And the grass so dry
we can take the short cut over the marshy field
to the village that sits tight against the wood.

Up and down the huge thighs of hills,
glancing between tree-legs at the city
across the river, glassy and grey-white,
in a ferment with its families,

veins of streets fluid with traffic,
people shimmering in and out
of markets, men on scaffolds, girls
stippled with light drifting from the hollows
of factories.

The pussy willow with its aluminium quiver.
And down by the deserted quarry
the sloe blossom out, the wild cherry.
All young, trembling in a passion

like the new milk, the first wet flower,
and all together, sick with the same desire.
Even the old man near death, staring out
of the cottage, his elbows quiet on the table.

STRAIGHT OUT

Straight out is a sunlit way of saying
What you really mean,
The world being what it is:
I mean the problem of burning clean.

Silence is a fine way of betraying
The stars men hang on trees.
Answers can be dangerous:
Saying nothing is bound to please.

Spring is a bloody time for doubting
The sweet juice of childhood,
Fingering the scars of paradise
On our way through the wood.

NOTHING ELSE WILL DO

Hating the night, my wife says —
Now we're on the downward grade:
from now on it's all downhill. . .

And I think of squandered years,
all the time spent in fury
just to reach this point,

sticking my neck out,
getting prepared
to step trembling from the egg.

A second birth.
All I can think of is the gift, the chance.
Nothing else will do.

I've been waiting for too long.
Even in my mother's womb
I sucked in the money-fear.

Poison was in the air —
bad food, ugly sex,
structures ready for every tree

where a life might blossom.
My youth knew it was rotten
to fix a price on living

but my father was right —
when I opened my mouth
a daft dribble ran down my chin.

One day I am going to howl.
Nothing else will do.
I promise fire of destruction

and a clean start from now.
Please forget my sad shadow
because in spite of love,

dear mother, I need to strip
naked and defenceless
and ripen in the sun.

CAT AND HOUSE

We need space.
The great luxury, deep hunger.
I plunge into the city to hunt for space;
meet the bank manager who blinks,
the estate agent with his switched-on smile.
I couldn't be greener.
The solicitor guides me
as if I'm blind, then waits for my instructions.
On the flat roof I feel stupid,
an actor facing an audience of chimney pots.
I drown in light.
Then I see the sea, the heave of headland,
half the city's choppy grey water
sliced up in streets — the surveyor
flapping his hands, angelic, fatherly,
asking me suddenly up there in space
what I do for a living.
I'm struck dumb.
Staring back pop-eyed I look over his shoulder
at fat clouds, bulging with life and no answers.

Head down I make for the bus,
blinded by property and the fear of it.
The young cat watches me,
Buddha-like in the wild grass of the wasteground.
Young enough to be nearly fearless,
coal-black with a white bib,
only its shoulders visible,
housed in grass and stationary as a stone.

It wasn't watching until I watched.
Next time it was there again.
How could it sit so still and look so quick?
I saw it once more, symbolic,

like a sign saying: *there's this!*
I was going in to sign the contract.

BLACK FLAG

I always felt cheated.
As a youth hungry for love,
feeding off myself,
I developed a terrible hard pride
on those lonely bike rides, at
those Leamington street corners.

I wanted the flesh of friendship,
the flesh of words,
real thighs under the skirts, breasts to knead,
always the heavy coarse wholemeal part
that my body was starved of. . .

Riding off with my father on Sundays
was a dumb pleasure,
helping him break the back
of that wartime allotment.
I didn't speak unless spoken to,
stamping on the spade
in a work rhythm, up and down the trench.
The solitude of carrots was good to imagine.
I liked to see the wet shoulders of cabbages,
to go freewheeling home in a crust of dirt
through the prim Sunday streets
with potato sacks shaggy on my handlebars.

I sank my tap root into that rented soil,
knowing I was bound to take off,
cheated of earth
and bitter with a father
who was too good, too innocent,
who eluded hate
the way he missed bullets in the war,
I admired him for his muteness,
his state of grace.

To see how ridiculous he was
I had to jump back inside my mother.

Crumbling between my fingers
their bread of love,
cheated by its whiteness —
that was the first step.
All my heroes were black, they were
full of dark power and distance.
Ill and hungry, thin with eating
the wrong food, I understood only one thing:
I could do nothing till I was ugly.

OLD WOMAN SINGING HYMNS

Everywhere you look, the old.
Mulish, vague, hanging their heads,
blowing and ashy-eyed,
croaking round in circles,
falling over in slow motion.
An old man in green checked wool,
face bloody as a sunset,
fingers so stained
you'd think he smoked tobacco direct from his hand.

So many old,
you feel they're all here
in the far west, the south,
like stones sunk to the bottom.
Old woman singing hymns under her breath.
Some so old
they can't remember who they are.
The traffic stamps round them in a war dance.
They wait helpless
like thrown-away clothes.
Shake them and their skin
would shower a rain of dry needles
like the dead undersides of gorse bushes.

Waxy heads, shrivelled lizard skins
worked over awkwardly
by the deplorable surgery of time,
ancient cabbage stalks rooted in tweeds and furs.
Lipless, hooded, knife-masked, crooked,
they stand far off, in a dim field of their own.
But shameless. They suck greedily at life.
My wife abhors them
with a woman's dread of disfigurement.
Old age, that sordid monkey!

I am getting ready for mine.
Come closer
any way you like!
I can shuffle and sing,
I'm a drop-out already.
Hear me spit and talk to myself,
listen to my idiot humming.
I feel a kinship with useless people
shuffling round without guilt.
There are many of us, many.

THREE WAYS OF CRYING

She used to cry
I want an orange, orange!
We played acrobats
where I lay spreadeagled
on the bed in the top room,
legs doubled like a grasshopper
and my feet a quaky platform
for my excited insect of a girl,
wriggling and squealing in mid-air,
who kept laughing, crying. . .
And such abandonment
as we collapsed sideways
and she cried *Again!*

I was thinking of the time,
left with her grandmother,
she opened her mouth awfully
like a fish,
blindly hiding her face.
Blind with pain and loss
I went away and was haunted
by that sudden baby spasm.
She was quite old, thirteen,
already skinny and tough.

Now she's older, beautiful,
tall as her mother
and she's outgrown so much,
so soon,
that her backbone's haughty with it.
She combs and combs her hair
to eliminate all childishness,
fringes her eyes with black
and now she's wicked enough
for the worst of this world.

Dreams play in her blood
and her mouth drains,
the curved bone of her nose
traces her young girl's contempt.

O haughty daughter,
ashamed of your birthday suit,
brooding over secrets, problems —
now you make us knock.
Now you cry in private
behind the door.

GOING AWAY

No blossom yet, but the blackthorn,
scoured and dried by a month of easterlies,
green blood set on fire by the drought,
will soon bring out its snow.
The white processions will excite the lanes.
Soon it will be spring.
Elm heads have a reddish glow,
the ash buds poke up hard and black on grey fingers,
swelling painfully
like my daughter's tender tits.

Now that it is definite
and we are really going,
it's strange: everything means much more.
I go out day by day pacing the old walks,
peering intently over hedges, eyes angled
like a camera at the cottage
from the high field where we took photographs
on some long ago picnic,
perched against the humming power pole
in the breezy heat,
the cows drifting near.

I have forgotten how old I am.
The air is sharp, sharp with millions of diamonds.
The cold March wind scythes at the sunlight.
I keep walking. I am light as a thistle.
And the wind blows in my blood,
the light washes through my thoughts;
I have mislaid the anguish of bonfires,
a farewell note flaring livid
on the mantelpiece that keeps saying
Don't try to follow me . . .
and the dead soot and silence
that bleeds, that has teeth,

27

that gnaws holes right through the heart.
Smash, smash!
It was the death
I smelled in the air
all my life
from the day I was born.

The sunlight splashes, the road so playfully
takes my feet, dropping me down
from the school on the corner
like the child I once was, running home.
Time storms, grass hides the scars,
I carry it all down in a rich silt,
the heart still not full, not done.
Going away, going home,
trampling and virginal
in the new womb of the calendar,
still not ready for death.

PRELUDE TO A PERFORMANCE

So this is what it means, the new freedom!
Here I go again — oh it's another guilty
Act of indecency, standing up there naked,
Scarred and fraudulent as my lecture notes. . .

To be an actor, that's it!
To pace like an exhibitionist
And blaze powerfully, give stupendous glances,
Live off the fat of my voice
Instead of hearing it, thin, streaky.

The train takes me: slippery with drizzle
It worms out over the viaducts,
The rivers, inlets, buries its brown length
In hillsides . . . hidden and hot like an intestine,
Where I sit sweating in a daydream
Of green fields terribly livid in the dirty daylight.

Then the burn of woods, above huddled, scabby
Cottages . . . a big house drowning in red ivy,
Going down for the last time in a waterlogged
Godforsaken meadow . . .
Drowning in Cornwall! I'd turn back,
Only this train is fixed and devilish,
A green bullish diesel changing gear like a bus.

Behind it, a strike boiling — up the line —
Scowling and black, bad weather.
It's not down here yet, says a passenger . . .
Good for Cornwall, bellows his wife
— And sounds drunk, huge, larger than life.
Jesus Christ, look, three of them — she's roaring it:
Three men to see off this tiny train . . .

I want to see her face, that deliberate, old mouth:
What a comfort, the great bourgeois din she makes!

I watch the grey floppy hat wobble — if I could snatch
It to cover the vile face of my cowardice.

Looping down over the harbour, iron-plated docks,
We land perched at the town edge,
Dead-end kids in a station that's unspeakable,
Peeling and so sad, the roof baring its bones
In a sugar of brown rust,
Walls filthy with discouragement
Like an out-of-order urinal.

And a taxi grabs me, the shiny grin of a Z-car
Gobbles me up — I loll back and go oozing,
Obscenely privileged, through the villas, bed-and-breakfast
Splendours — the steep streets filling with workers
Bent honest and agonized over handlebars,
Revving themselves back to loaf-houses, parsnip-wives . . .

Proudly the taximan steers me through
The tilted labyrinth of his unbeatable rainy town.
Now it won't be long — soon the money-need
Will drag me out all of a shiver
From the warm water, the tinkling orange-and-blue café —

I shall start gabbling wildly into cold silence,
Smiling at young faces, watering them with smiles —
— And such sunlight, from a totally imagined eloquence!

I'll see hope everywhere — a mere giggle will save me —
Or be suddenly crucified by a choked laugh, by
A fluorescent that dims and stutters in the building opposite.

A DEATH IN THE FAMILY

Never leaving or marrying,
A stubborn solitary all his life,
hardly a word and never laughing aloud,
my uncle slips out of the world
just like going next door.

Suddenly he is dead,
dead as Coventry, dead as that music,
his tucked violin, his fat cello:
I would love to see him again
safe at home in the paraffin smell,
fuddled with sleep and shirt-sleeved . . .

Young man at the breakfast table,
the paper propped, the hand groping,
and his mother tuts as she watches,
dying to be of use —
my old hovering grandmother.

So she gives the fire a rattle
for the last of her sons,
the pale hollowed young eater
who will slip through her love
all thin and shadowy
letting nobody come close,

afraid of everything in his quiet way.
I want to know one thing:
what his mates thought of him
in the factory that lifetime.
One place. One death. One secret.

He taught me how to swim
and he taught my brother.
Before leaving he used to weigh himself.

He bought us lavish boxes of fireworks
and we ran his errands.

He let me ride his bike
while he steamed his nose
drinking tea and talk in our house.
Once I saw an old snap of him:
very frightened and caught,
a frail boy in a big collar and frilly clothes.

I WANT TO LIVE

Break silence wave goodbye
It's my birthday
The sun rolls the comet runs on
Another forty thousand years
The stars shoot
One two
I don't wish I want
Life's grim I want to live

The blue and the yellow wine
Of burning bright
October
Robes me each noon
And today again a warm pale
Sunny birthday suit
Reminds me I want to live

My child makes me a card
Next morning
There it is on the table:
I am sending greetings true
From us to you
We are so near
Our love forever
In your keeping
And I smile shaking with life with tears

I want to live
My wife has a gallstone
That's life
Wormwood and gall
She's afraid and she feels alone
At the hospital
Gold October in a window
She'll want to live

What use am I
The earth rolls like our dog

Joyful in the sun
Twisting on its back
Through space
In the sun on the fishquay
In the Admiral McBride
I sit tight and smile drinking

Happy birthday
I am forty-one
I want to live forever
Nobody believes in death
Not for them
I want to live better than this
One day.

ENCOUNTER

Nothing in common
except some days and years
stuck in the same office

they meet on the pavement
outside the Ladies',
the older man's bald head

afloat in sunlight,
bobbing up and down
as he talks

against the raw cliff
of the new college —
chafed at the base

by a river of traffic.
The river slides and screeches,
making them wince

the older man feels sick
so he's going home.
His friend stands exhausted

the weather lovely,
the wife bustling out
into the light, blinking

nothing in common
except the sun touching lightly
an encroaching weariness.

ANOTHER COUNTRY

Under the sweating arch of the bridge,
before we even see them
we can hear yells
from their playground.
And we know it's theirs
as we move in closer
on our huge legs, two Gullivers.

Swings are rooted
behind the council houses,
green stilts in a patch of tarmac
alongside the railway bank.
The shrieks, clashing chains
die down
for us to enter the arena.

One girl, about six,
has a face like an Eskimo.
Shy in front of the camera
she shuts her eyes,
thinking we can't see her.
Now she's a dead bird.
A boy dances on the curve
of a concrete pipe
while his brother stands tiptoe
to peer through a brick porthole.

Grinning and waving, we walk off,
promising pictures all round.
Even acting they're more natural than us.

THE VILLAGE

The Pakistanis who work for him
he calls boys.
They all come from
the same village;
and because their English is poor
they look to him,
more an uncle than a boss,
more a guardian than either.

The restaurant is their village.
When you visit it
they flash a smile
across the fence of language.
In the dappled light
by the counter
they are voluble, rapid, really themselves,
waiting for you to go.
The guardian watches.
He arrives home after midnight
and rises late, even
later now because he is married
to a woman he calls
Princess of the Sleeping Kingdom.

THE POET

Don't say
'you'd be better off
without wife or kids
people like you
never ought to get married'

Don't tell me
'you'd be quite happy
in some crumbling slum
or else on the move
a day-to-day liver
opening the doors of dreams
wandering through all moony
like a tit in a trance'

A lot of freedom bothers me
like a lot of beard or long hair
I'm a special case without that
I want to be in the clutches
like everyone else
I want common joys
like food
money in my pocket
clean socks
bills and bookshelves
I want to know what it feels like
it's very lonely being special
I want the lot
the full catastrophe
and that's what I've got.

JOY STREET

Come in the morning early;
Leave the war of the world.

Hang from the bus window
And wave eagerly
When you see me.

Let the sky in you
Flow into your face.
Now you make it new.

Bring the seeds for sowing,
Joys of fatherhood:
Plant them in a circle,
Sweet peas, shirley poppies . . .
Shake them in your pocket,
The flower sounds of love.

Young shoots in the cities,
Burst through the concrete.
Be as good as your dreams.

When you feel glad
It doesn't matter.
You can live for ever
Or die tomorrow.

Come in the morning early,
Before the waste of the day.

IT'S YOURS

This is the time to say it.
The typewriter never lies.
Nobody made me cringe,
the tears were all mine,
I went slinking down the street
under the same dead sky
like something dirty that was
born in a cage.
Didn't they expect it?
How else could I have got the idea
that the world was private,
you had to wipe your feet
and smile apologetically
like entering a hotel
you couldn't really afford?

Now there is no problem.
The revolving door accomplishes the revolution.
Walk up and push. March in.
The instant you realise it belongs to you
it's yours. Take it over.
Swagger through every room
blithe as a savage
and say goodbye, stuff it,
I don't want it after all.
Goodbye goodbye.
All I need is me.
And goodbye humble pie.